CW00843010

The Monster that Came in from the Cold!

A Dark Chronicles of Weston super Mare story

Volume 1

© Ade Bowen 2023

Cover design by Ade Bowen

Published in the United Kingdom by Big Pussycat Publications.

www.bigpussycatpublications.com
Tel: 01934 620959
www.facebook.com/bigcatpublications
Print Edition ISBN: 9798863913636
Ebook Edition: 978-1-7398265-2-9
First printed 2023

The Monster that came in from the Cold

A Dark Chronicles of Weston super Mare story

Written by Ade Bowen

Contents

Introduction

Hello

I am the Ghoul of Cool, your storyteller of these terror-ific tales. I collect stories from the darker side of Weston's history and re-tell them here for your..... entertainment.

Inside you will discover stories that will send shivers down your spine. Your knees will knock and your heart pump faster as you turn each freighting good page.

The Autumn Monster is a Weston legend that dates back 100 years. In the Autumn, when the days start getting shorter, it is not just spiders that come in out of the cold.

This book also included, chapter one of 'The Curse of the Full Moon', a story from 'Dark Chronicles of Weston super Mare', Volume 1

Read this on your own with the lights down low,

if you dare!

Autumn Monster, Autumn Monster
with your eyes so wide.
I know it is cold out
and it's so warm inside.
Here is some cake and milk
to keep you warm.
Please stay in the garden
and mean us no harm.

The Monster that Came in from the Cold

Chapter One

"Is Granddad OK?" I asked Nana when I went to visit them up on the hill in Worlebury, a beautiful community overlooking Weston Bay one side and Sand Bay the other.

"Yes, dear, he is fine. But why do you ask?"

"He told me something really weird," I answered. We were sitting in my grandparents' living room. The wallpaper and furniture were exactly as you would expect your grandparents' living room to look like. There were frills on the bottom of the sofa. There were frills on the lamp shade. There were frills on the coffee table. Even the cat's collar had homemade frills on it. The house had lots of frills, but not many thrills. Or so I thought!

Nana gave me the 'go on' look, so I continued.

"When I was talking to him yesterday, he said God was watching over him."

She gave me the look again, but with a more serious tone. "Go on."

"Granddad told me that, every time he wakes up in the night to go to the toilet, God switches the light on for him, and when he finishes, God switches the light off again. What does that mean?"

Nana looked at me. "Darling, it means your silly Granddad is weeing in the fridge again."

I was visiting my grandparents for the weekend. Mum and Dad were away on a 'dirty weekend' as they called it, which I could only imagine meant they were playing with mud, so I was staying with my mum's mum and dad in Worlebury for the weekend. It is nice here. The view over Sand Bay is fab, but best of all is being able to play in the woods.

"Nana, can I go play in the woods please?"

Nana looked at her watch, looked out the window and frowned. "No dear. It is going to be dark soon and the Autumn Monster will be out."

"What Autumn Monster?" It was late September. The days were getting shorter and the colours in the leaves made the trees look like the patchwork quilt that hung on the bottom of the bed in the spare room. The bedroom where I slept when visiting.

"Your mother never told you about the Autumn Monster? That is very remiss of her. Come, sit and I will tell you." Nana gestured for me to sit next to her by patting the frilly cushion next to her on the two-seater sofa. I picked up the cushion, sat down and gave the cushion a hug.

"Have you ever noticed that there are always more spiders in the house in autumn?"

"Yeah. Dad says it is because they like watching Strictly Come Dancing on TV."

"Ha. No. Well, that may be true, but mostly it is because, when it starts getting cold in the autumn, spiders come in looking for somewhere warm. Well, it is not just spiders that come in out of the cold. So does the Autumn Monster.

"During the summer it lives deep in the woods, but come the colder autumn days, when the nights draw in and the leaves turn red, the Autumn Monster likes to seek the warmth of human houses. Back when I was young, we used to leave a bowl of warm milk out in the night and a slice of autumn cake. We believed that would keep it out of our houses."

Nana thought Granddad was weird for having a wee in the fridge, and here she is telling me stories of monsters.

"Can we leave some autumn cake and hot milk out for the monster tonight please Nana?" OK, I didn't really believe in Autumn Monsters, but I did like Nana's cake – and there is nothing wrong with being careful, is there?

Is there?

Chapter Two

We spent the rest of the evening making autumn cake and it smelt delicious. While it was cooling down, I got ready for bed, put my jimjams on and sat with Granddad watching Strictly Come Dancing.

As I watched some celebrity I had never heard of fall over in his rehearsal, I felt a tickle on my leg. I looked down. Crawling up my leg was the biggest spider I have ever seen. Its legs were hairy, its body was big and bulbous and its eyes were staring right back at me. I am sure I saw its mouth say "Yum yum!" but I may have imagined that.

I was not proud of my reaction. I jumped up, screamed and scared my granddad, who spluttered and his false teeth fell out. "W-w-what is it?" he asked, grabbing the side of the frilly armchair and looking at me with concern.

Jumping up and down and wiggling my leg around I yelped, "Spider. There is a big spider on my leg."

"Oh. Hold still child and let me have a look," he asked.

I tried my best to calm down and let Granddad have a look.

"Oh, he is a big one. There is enough meat on him for us all to have a leg for Sunday roast. Stay still." With that,

Granddad put his hand on my knee and let the spider climb onto his hand. I backed away in fear, but Granddad just giggled and said, "Come one biggie. I'm afraid you will have to make your web outside tonight." He opened the window and let the spider out. Closing the window, Granddad opened his hand to show me. "See, all gone. You know, I used to have a pair of trousers made from spider silk. I had to return them though. The fly kept getting stuck. Good job it was not the Autumn Monster. I would have had to get the newspaper out. Then you would have been proper scared."

Nana called me. "Come on dear. It is time to put the hot milk and cake out for the Autumn Monster, then bed time."

Nana let me carry the cake as we went outside. She put the hot milk down on a little metal table in the corner of the garden and I put the cake down next to it.

"Now we sing the song," said Nana.

"There is a song?"

Nana smiled at me. "Yes, there is always a song." She sat on her garden bench and gestured for me to sit next to her again by patting the space next to her. "To let the Autumn Monster know we mean it no harm, along with the gift of milk and autumn cake, we always sing the

Autumn Monster song, and that means it will leave us alone. It goes like this.

"Autumn Monster, Autumn Monster with your eyes so wide.
I know it is cold out and it's so warm inside.
Here is some cake and milk to keep you warm.
Please stay in the garden and mean us no harm."

We sang it together, left the warm milk and autumn cake in the garden and headed inside. As we walked back indoors, I looked back at the milk and cake. I could have sworn I saw something moving in the bushes out of the corner of my eye, but when I looked straight at it, there was nothing there.

Chapter Three

When we got back inside, Nana sliced up cake for us all and we sat and watched the rest of Strictly while eating autumn cake and sipping warm milk. It was yummy! The sticky golden syrup, nuts and raisins worked well together, and the sprinkling of sugar on the top was delicious.

Granddad looked at me and said, "You know this is monster cake?"

"Nana said it is called autumn cake," I answered. Well, I actually said, "Mema mag ip ip warum kak," because my mouth was full, but Granddad knew what I meant. He used to be a dentist.

He continued. "Yes, yes. Its official name is autumn cake, but growing up in Worlebury, we always knew it as monster cake because it is what you left for the monster. Speaking of monsters, you know Albert Einstein?"

"Isn't he the clever man?" I guessed, a bit unsure.

"Yes, the clever man. Albert Einstein was very clever, but his brother, Frank was a monster!"

Chapter Four

After that, it was sleepy time. I got into bed, but I was not tired. Even over the taste of the toothpaste, I could still taste the autumn cake, and I wanted more.

I slipped out of bed as quietly as I could and crept to my bedroom door. Peering through the half open door, I could see Nana and Granddad playing cards on the dining room table. On the surface beyond that was the rest of the cake. There was no way I could get past them to the cake without them seeing me, but there was another slice of cake in the garden! I thought of the cake going to waste out there when it could have been in my belly and I made a decision.

That cake would be mine!

There was no real Autumn Monster anyhow. I was sure it was just something that my grandparents had made up, like the Sergeant Major Granddad said lived under the table and ate the crumbs, or the sock fairy that tidies up socks every night.

So I carefully opened my window and snuck outside. My grandparents owned a bungalow, so luckily I could just step out, not climb down a wall. Making as little noise as I could, I crept around to the front garden, ducking under the living room window, and commando crawled my way to the table where we had left the cake and milk. The cake and milk were still there. Of course they were still there. It was not like there was a real monster going to eat the cake and drink the milk. I grabbed the cake and snuggled up to the bush to keep out of sight, but it was cold. Cold, and dark. Cold and dark and there were strange noises coming from beyond the garden bushes.

I don't like the cold. I am not fond of the dark. I definitely am not keen on strange noises.

I decided that being outside was a silly idea, so I headed back to my bedroom window with the cake as quietly as possible. In the dark I didn't see a spider web. I walked straight into it with my mouth open. It may look like candy floss – but it sure does not taste like candy floss.

After quickly peeling the sticky web out of my hair with one hand, I climbed back in. Safely back indoors, I shut the window and tiptoed back to check on my grandparents. They were still playing cards and had not seemed to notice my little adventure outdoors.

I let out a sign of breath that I had not realised I had been holding and tiptoed back into bed. More cake for me! Yes, it was a bit damp from the night air. Yes, there was a bit of grass I had to pick off it, but cake is cake. I quietly crawled into bed and made a tent under the duvet. Sat crossed legged with my head under the bedclothes, I scoffed the cake and picked up the crumbs before lying down and drifting off to sleep.

Chapter Five

I woke up some time later to a weird scuffling noise. It sounded like a half full plastic bag being dragged over dry leaves by lots of tired snakes. The light from the living room was off, so I guessed it must be late and my grandparents had gone to sleep. So what had been making the noise? It had stopped now, so I closed my eyes and tried to get back to sleep.

That idea did not last 10 seconds before there was the same weird scuffling noise again. I sat up to try and get a bearing on it. Where was it coming from? To my horror, the sound was coming from inside the house. I quickly drew the duvet over my head. Everybody knows that the strongest thing in the world is duvet covers, I would be safe here – but did monsters know that?

The same weird scuffling noise disturbed my thoughts, followed by a quiet thud, like something big trying to be very quiet. Dragging the duvet with me for protection, I tiptoed up to my bedroom door and peeked through the opening. It was still dark, but there was enough moonlight coming through the window that I could see the shape of something in the kitchen.

The shape of something huge.

I picked up my mobile phone and poked at it until I found the torch app. Suddenly, everything was flooded in light. I could now clearly see the monster that stood in the kitchen trying to carefully take the lid off my nana's cake tin.

It had lots of legs like a skittering spider, which floated and waved all around.

It had a big round body and a big fat head that the legs kept high off the ground.

On top of its head, sitting proud as can be, was a horn like a unicorn's got.

Its two big round eyes seemed to meet in the middle and were green, the same colour as snot.

It smelt like dry leaves that go crunch under foot mixed with smells I would rather forget.

But its teeth were enormous, like stalactites dangling, with a mouth that was cave like and wet.

It was huge, it was shocking, it should not be here, the worst thing that I ever will see.

I stood there all shaken, pinned to the spot and I let out a small bit of wee.

I stared at it. Its eyes shifted between me and the cake tin. Slowly but surely, it prized the lid off the cake tin. The lid fell to the ground with a crash. I looked away to my phone and opened the camera app. The monster had one of its long arms in the tin. I pointed the camera at the monster and took a photo. It lifted the cake out of the tin and put it on the table. I opened the WhatsApp app and flicked to the group chat with my school friends. It found a knife and cut off a big slice of cake. I sent the photo of the monster to my friends. It ate the cake.

As it was wiping cake crumbs off its face, my granddad came out of his bedroom doing up his dressing robe. "What are you doing up at this hour banging and crashing about?" he asked.

Open mouthed, I just pointed at the Autumn Monster, who was carefully putting the lid back on the cake tin, looking a bit sheepish.

Granddad took in the scene of the monster in his kitchen.

"Oi, what are you doing in here? Your cake is outside on the table," he said in a surprisingly calm tone.

In response, the monster shook its head and pointed one of its long arms at me. It then made an 'eating' mime with two of its other arms.

Granddad looked at me. The monster gave me a hard stare. I wanted to lie, but looking down at my PJs I also still had cake crumbs on me. I had been caught red handed and crumb covered.

"I may have snuck out and eaten the cake we left for the monster," I admitted.

"You silly thing. I now have to go grab a newspaper and shoo this thing out the house before your nana wakes up." Granddad picked up the newspaper from the table, rolled it into a tube and started waving it at the monster.

"Shoo, go on. Get your creepy legs out of my house. You have had your cake. Go on. Out of it!"

To my surprise, it worked. The Autumn Monster turned around and retreated out the house before the waving of the newspaper. At the door it stopped, looked straight at me and moved two tentacles from its eyes to pointing at me and back. Clearly, it wanted me to know it would be watching me. With a click of the door closing, it had gone.

Granddad turned to me and said, "Now, get yourself back to bed. Don't eat the Autumn Monster's share of the cake again, and whatever you do, don't tell your nana about this."

Chapter Six

In the morning, I woke up around 8am, got dressed and left my room. I was half convinced that last night had only been a dream. I mean, the sight of my granddad in his jimjams shooing off a multi legged monster with a rolled up newspaper seem absurd.

Nana was up and had left a multi packet of cereal on the table for me to choose from. Granddad came to join me and we shared a knowing glance as he sat down. Just as he picked up his newspaper, Nana shouted.

"Oi! Which of you two has been at my Autumn Cake?"

Granddad looked at me. I looked at him. Smiles broke out on our faces and we laughed while Nana looked at us both like we had lost our marbles.

When I stopped laughing and Nana had wandered off, I turned to Granddad and said, "Granddad, you were so brave last night with the Autumn Monster, shooing him away with just a newspaper. Were you not afraid?"

"Ha. No – I was not afraid. I knew something you didn't."

"What? What did you know?"

"Well, yesterday was Saturday. I knew I was safe, because the Autumn Monster only eats people on Chewsday!"

Autumn Cake

If you want to keep the Autumn Monster away from your house, here is how to make your own Autumn Cake. The cake is nutty, fruity and great with warm honey milk.

WARNING – Contains NUTS

Ingredients

250 g butter or Stork
200 g castor sugar
190 g self raising flour (or 95 g of self raising flour and 95 g of chestnut flour if you can get it).
2 teaspoon baking powder
1 teaspoon salt
2 eggs, lightly beaten
¼ cup of milk
2 teaspoons of vanilla extract
140 g chopped chestnuts
140 g chopped pecan nuts (optional)
Raisins, as many as you like
Golden syrup

Instructions

1. Pre heat the oven to 160 C and lightly flour your baking tins.

2. Sift the flour, salt and baking powder. Chop the chestnuts. Make sure the pieces are no larger than a pea.

3. Lightly beat the eggs and add the vanilla in a bowl. In a mixing bowl, cream the butter and sugar until light and fluffy.

4. Add the egg mixture a little at a time to the butter/sugar. Then add half the flour, then milk, then rest of the flour. Add the ground chestnuts and pecan nuts and combine.

5. Pour in the golden syrup, do not mix.

6. Transfer the cake batter mixture into the baking tin. Bake for 30-35 minutes or until a skewer comes out clean. Add a sprinkle of sugar to the top.

From the pages of

Dark Chronicles of Weston super Mare

The Curse of the Full Moon

Following are the first two chapters of the first story from Dark Chronicles of Weston Super Mare.

To read the full story, plus two other spooky stories, order your copy from Amazon.

Introduction

The modern Weston super Mare is well known for its miles of beaches, its donkeys and its fish and chips, but dig deeper and you will find there are some places you would wish to avoid, especially on a full moon.

In 1843, Weston super Mare was a small seaside village that was quickly growing due to the arrival of Isambard Kingdom Brunel's train line. Shops and hotels were rapidly being built to accommodate the new tourist trade and normally there was an open house or inn that would provide accommodation for the right price.

Normally it is, but not on this fateful night. This is the story of when a holiday for two young children from Bath went horribly wrong.

Chapter One

When Charlie and Delilah arrived on a horse drawn train on a crisp, clear October evening, Uncle Christopher was not there to meet them as arranged. The horses brought the carriages into Weston after they were detached from steam trains at the main line junction in Bristol. The children dragged their luggage from the sparsely populated carriage and pulled it across the exposed platform of the station to wait patiently outside the station. The breeze from the sea had a cold edge to it, and the two siblings sat together to try and keep warm.

"He must have been delayed leaving the farm." 12-year-old Charlie told Delilah, giving her a big hug to reassure her. Delilah was 3 years younger than her brother, and he was very good at looking after her. That was why they had been allowed to travel on their own from Bath to visit their uncle.

Delilah held her teddy tighter and looked into Charlie's eyes. "I'm scared Charlie. I don't like it here."

"Do not worry. Uncle Christopher will be here."

Charlie looked up the street again, willing Uncle Christopher's horse and cart to appear around the corner. Uncle Christopher and Auntie Nelly owned a big farmhouse in Banwell and every year Charlie and Delilah would come to visit for a month. Charlie would help in the fields, and Delilah would play with Auntie Nell as she made cakes in the big kitchen.

They had been waiting for almost half an hour when movement caught Charlie's eye in the shadow of an alleyway. Something that looked like a large dog emerged into the evening twilight. The creature stopped and stared straight at Charlie, before sulking into the darkness.

Charlie looked back at his sister, shivering in the cold wind. He made a decision. "Come on; let's find something to eat and drink. I will leave a message with the station manager for Uncle Christopher to let him know we will be back in an hour, and then we can get some food in your belly. That will cheer you up"

After leaving a note with the station manager, Charlie grabbed their baggage and headed into town. Not many places were open this late in the season, and those that were, did not welcome two young strangers on this crisp evening.

At the third open pub, Charlie and Delilah pleaded with the landlord. "Please, we have no money, but our uncle will pay when he arrives. We just need some soup and a warm place to wait."

"You don't really expect me to believe that do you, street scum. Get out and be on your way!" was the mean response given.

By the time the sun had set, they found themselves stood in front of an odd-looking terraced building in Orchard Street. This wide fronted property was twice the size of its neighbours and looked like some kind of storage facility. It looked deserted, except for flickering candlelight in an upstairs window. Its wide double door was ajar, and Charlie decided they would quickly shelter here then go back to the station to surely find Uncle Christopher waiting. A full moon was rising in the east, casting dark blue shadows across the street. Charlie thought he saw another dark dog like creature watching him from the back of a shop, but when he looked straight at it, there was nothing. 'Just the shadows playing tricks with my imagination' he convinced himself as he pushed the door open to let Delilah in before grabbing the luggage and pulling it through the door.

Chapter Two

Inside, it was dark and gloomy, but at least it gave shelter from the wind.

"Hello?" Charlie called out. "Is there anybody here?"

The front door slammed shut and Delilah screamed. Charlie joined the scream and he spun round, fists up, ready to defend his sister. There was nothing there.

"Must have been the wind blowing the door shut behind us." Charlie reasoned, and he moved to give his sister a hug. "Don't worry. We will just warm up here. Five-minutes out of the wind won't kill us."

Won't it Charlie? Are you sure?

The room they were in revealed itself to be some kind of large storage area. White sheets were draped over everything, and a thin layer of dust covered the sheets. Charlie walked deeper into the room and discovered a kitchen, but found the larder bare. He called to his sister. "It looks like this place has been empty for a while." He walked over to a water jug on a dusty table that was lit by the full moon outside and picked it up. There was about a pint of water at the bottom. After opening a couple of cobweb covered cupboards, he found some abandoned cups. He turned back and screamed as a pair of canine eyes observed him hungrily through the window.

"Charlie. What is it? Are you OK?"

Charlie blinked, and the eyes were gone. He called back to his sister. "It is ok. I just thought I saw something. Trick of the light I guess." Still, he decided to stay away from the window and forfeit the drink for now. Just in case.

Charlie returned to his sister, picked up the luggage and turned towards the stairs. "Let's see if there is some food."

Leading the way, he climbed the stairs. Each step creaked under their weight. He stopped after three steps to check on Delilah, but heard a fourth footstep creak on the stairs. Weird. Delilah was right behind him, so he set off again. Creak, creak, creak. He stopped again to get a better grip on the luggage, and heard another creak, another footstep.

"Charlie, I don't like it here." Delilah spoke in a whisper from behind him.

Charlie put on a brave voice, much braver than he was feeling inside. "It's OK. We will only stay here a short while. Uncle Christopher will be here for us soon, I promise."

At the top of the stairs was a window, and through it, the full moon could be seen clearly in the cloudless night sky. As they climbed the stairs, Charlie saw a shadow crossed the window out the corner of his eye. He stopped to look up, but could only see the full moon casting its light on the rooftops opposite. The stairs gave an extra creak again. Charlie gave the luggage another heave and reached the top of the stairs. Wiping his brow, he turned to help his sister up the stairs, but she was not there. She had disappeared.

Find out what happens to Charlie and Delilah in Dark Chronicles of Weston super Mare, volume 1.

Printed in Great Britain
by Amazon

39728959R00020